# What Do You Want to Be?

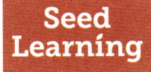

# pilot

# doctor

# dancer

# baker

# astronaut

# teacher

# musician

# firefighter

# What do you want to be?

# I want to be a pilot.

# What do you want to be?

# I want to be a dancer.

# What do you want to be?

# I want to be a doctor.

# What do you want to be?

# I want to be a baker.

# What do you want to be?

# I want to be a teacher.

# What do you want to be?

*Lalalalala!* I want to be a musician.

# Let's learn more about Italy.

Gelato